W9-BGJ-152

ROCKS AND MINERALS

Please visit our web site at: **www.garethstevens.com**
For a free color catalog describing Gareth Stevens Publishing's list of high-quality books and multimedia programs, call 1-800-542-2595 (USA) or 1-800-387-3178 (Canada). Gareth Stevens Publishing's fax: (414) 332-3567.

Library of Congress Cataloging-in-Publication Data available upon request from publisher. Fax (414) 336-0157 for the attention of thePublishing Records Department.

ISBN 0-8368-3384-8

This edition first published in 2004 by
Gareth Stevens Publishing
A World Almanac Education Group Company
330 West Olive Street, Suite 100
Milwaukee, WI 53212 USA

This U.S. edition copyright © 2004 by Gareth Stevens, Inc. First published in 2000 as *Solid: The Rocks & Minerals Files* by Discovery Enterprises, LLC, Bethesda, Maryland. © 2000 by Discovery Communications, Inc.

Further resources for students and educators available at
www.discoveryschool.com

Designed by Bill SMITH STUDIO
Creative Director: Ron Leighton
Designers: Sonia Gauba, Nick Stone, Dmitri Kushnirsky, Bill Wilson, Darren D'Agostino, Joe Bartos
Photo Editors: Jennifer Friel, Scott Haag
Art Buyers: Paula Radding, Marianne Tozzo

Gareth Stevens Editor: Betsy Rasmussen
Gareth Stevens Art Director: Tammy Gruenewald
Technical Advisor: Emily Watson

Printed in the United States of America

1 2 3 4 5 6 7 8 9 08 07 06 05 04

Writer: Anna Prokos

Editor: Anna Prokos

Photographs: p. 3: (top right) & p. 28: (left), Florence Bascom Sophia Smith Collection/Smith College; (bottom left) globe, MapArt; p. 5: hornblende © Biophoto Associate/Photo Researchers, Inc.; p 4–5 Green Mtn quarry © A.J. Copley/Visuals Unlimited; p. 8–9 all photos © PhotoDisc; p. 10: (top) fluorite [white light & UV light] © Dr. Ed Degginger; (bottom) fluorite [regular & phosphorescent] © 2000 sHINICHI kato; p. 11: (top) quartz © Charles D. Winter/Photo Researchers, Inc.; (center) thermoluminescence © Astrid &

Hanns-Frieder Michler/Science Photo Library/Photo Researchers, Inc.; p. 29: (top right) Florence Bascom with group Sophia Smith Collection/Kolb Brothers Grand Canyon; (bottom left) Florence Bascom at Yellowstone Lake Sophia Smith Collection/Smith College; p. 30: (top) scales Digital Stock; (center) diamond © PhotoDisc.

Illustrations: p. 24-25: cafeteria tray, Chris Burke; p. 26–27: rock discovery, Lee MacLeod.

Acknowledgments: p. 14, Gold, Boys, Gold! Courtesy Museum of the City of San Francisco; p. 28–29 background information for Florence Bascom, http://geodlio.st.usm.edu/fbascom.html.

CONTENTS

Do you have rocks in your head? You will after you read this Discovery Channel book. That's because ROCKS and MINERALS is all about the very solid matter that makes up Earth.

There's no such thing as a plain old rock. In fact, every rock tells a story. And at least one component in every rock has been on Earth since Earth formed. You could say any rock is a piece of history. Rocks tell us a story: about where it formed, what it's made of, and where it's been. They even give us clues as to what's going on below Earth's rocky surface. Minerals are just as important—rocks are composed of them. Without minerals, rocks wouldn't exist.

So put on your stone face for a rocking journey through the rock cycle.

ROCKS AND MINERALS

Florence Bascom, the first woman geologist in the United States. See page 28.

Final Project

3

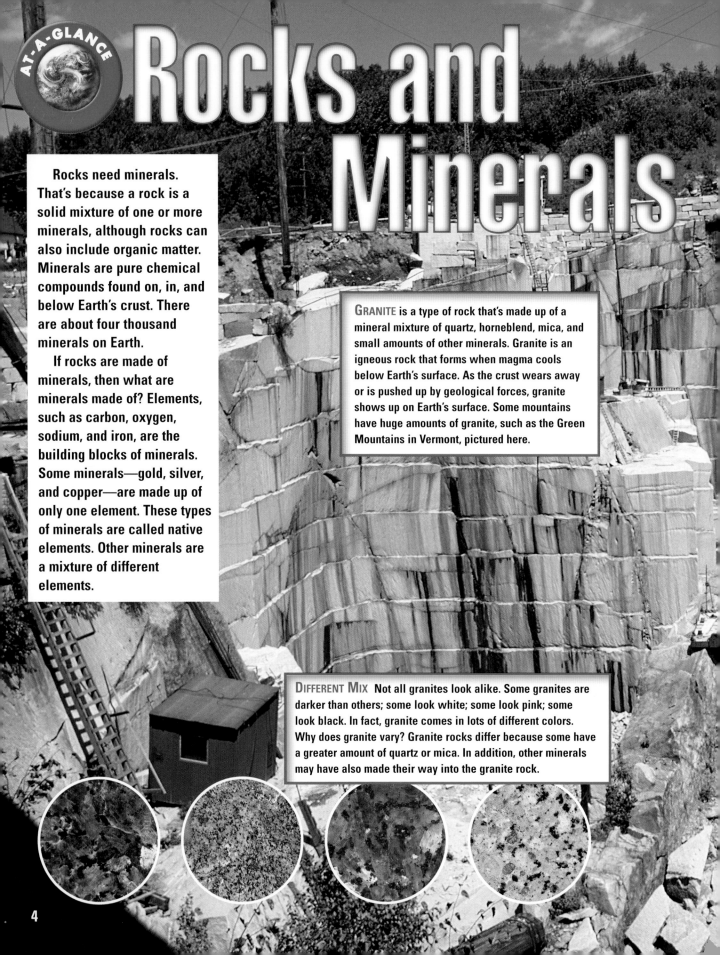

Rocks and Minerals

Rocks need minerals. That's because a rock is a solid mixture of one or more minerals, although rocks can also include organic matter. Minerals are pure chemical compounds found on, in, and below Earth's crust. There are about four thousand minerals on Earth.

If rocks are made of minerals, then what are minerals made of? Elements, such as carbon, oxygen, sodium, and iron, are the building blocks of minerals. Some minerals—gold, silver, and copper—are made up of only one element. These types of minerals are called native elements. Other minerals are a mixture of different elements.

GRANITE is a type of rock that's made up of a mineral mixture of quartz, horneblend, mica, and small amounts of other minerals. Granite is an igneous rock that forms when magma cools below Earth's surface. As the crust wears away or is pushed up by geological forces, granite shows up on Earth's surface. Some mountains have huge amounts of granite, such as the Green Mountains in Vermont, pictured here.

DIFFERENT MIX Not all granites look alike. Some granites are darker than others; some look white; some look pink; some look black. In fact, granite comes in lots of different colors. Why does granite vary? Granite rocks differ because some have a greater amount of quartz or mica. In addition, other minerals may have also made their way into the granite rock.

QUARTZ One element in granite, called quartz, is the most common mineral on Earth's surface. Depending on how quickly it cools and the other matter found with it, quartz can be clear, white, or rose-colored. Amethyst, the birthstone for February, is also quartz, but amethyst's chemical composition makes it purple.

HORNBLENDE Hornblende is a dark green mineral whose crystals appear fiberlike. This mineral is common in many other kinds of rocks besides granite, such as basalt, diorite, schist, and gneiss (nice). A close relative of hornblende is asbestos, another mineral with a fibrous structure. Asbestos fibers, unlike hornblende fibers, can cause lung cancer in humans.

MICA Another element in granite is mica. Micas usually form in the shape of flakes, shreds, or scales. The most common type of mica in granite is called muscovite mica. It can be clear, white, gray, or brown. It's almost transparent, so it's responsible for the twinkling or sparkling appearance of granite. Muscovite mica is so clear that people in Moscow, Russia, once used it as a substitute for glass. You can also find mica in paints, plastics, and roofing materials.

Take Me for Granite

Q: We're talking with a piece of granite about its life. Is it a hard life, Gran?

A: You bet it's hard. Especially when you're an igneous rock, like yours truly.

Q: Did you say, ignorant rock?

A: I beg your pardon! I said igneous rock. You know—as in ignite.

Q: Ignite—as in start a fire?

A: You got it. Igneous rocks are sometimes called fire rocks. We're made when magma or lava cools off and hardens.

Q: Magma OR lava? I thought they were the same thing.

A: They're both names for melted minerals. But we use the word magma when the molten minerals are below Earth's surface and lava when they're on or above Earth's surface. So there are two kinds of igneous rocks: those formed beneath Earth's surface and those formed above it.

Q: Do the two kinds look the same?

A: Not exactly. If you look at an intrusive igneous rock, like yours truly, one formed inside the hot Earth, you can see large mineral grains. That's because it takes a long time to cool off down there, and my crystals can grow bigger. During the slow hardening process, minerals arrange themselves into large crystals, or grains.

Q: How about the other kind? What do you call them?

A: Well, if **in**trusive igneous rocks are formed **in** Earth by magma, what would you call igneous rocks that are formed **ex**ternally, outside of Earth?

Q: Uh . . . excellent? Extreme?

A: No, they're called **ex**trusive igneous rocks. And they look different because they start to cool the instant lava is exposed to air and moisture. Their minerals have no time to make large crystals. That's why the rocks look fine-grained, smooth, and even.

Q: I see. Do you ever wish you could come up to the surface and hang out with the extrusive branch of your family?

A: I do come up—all the time! Intrusive igneous rocks are continually being pushed up to the surface. Of course, it takes a long time. But that's OK. What else have I got to do? Nothing's more patient than a rock.

Q: How do you spend your time when you surface?

A: Well, there are a lot of relatives to visit. As a group, igneous rocks make up about 95 percent of the upper part of Earth's crust.

Q: Wow! How does it feel, hanging out on top of Earth?

A: I could have a breakdown. Literally. With enough weathering by the wind, rain, and waves, I could get broken down into fine little pieces, little grains called sediments. When I'm broken down enough, I could become a new rock.

Q: Really? What kind of new rock? Another igneous one?

A: Nope. All my little pieces will get moved by the wind and waves and eventually get deposited as sediments. Sediments are bits and pieces of minerals, rocks, plants, and even parts of dead animals that pile up in water. Those pieces are compacted and cemented over time to form a sedimentary rock, like sandstone. And that would be the beginning of a whole new life.

Q: How so?

A: As granite, I'm strong. I'm capable. I can stand up to almost anything, and people take advantage of that. They use igneous rocks like granite for making all sorts of stuff, such as buildings and monuments. The Vietnam Veterans Memorial in Washington, D.C., is made up of 150 panels of black granite.

Q: And sedimentary rocks don't get used that way?

A: Nope. They're often too soft. But what they're really good at is telling stories. Sedimentary rocks such as sandstone are filled with mounds of information about Earth's history. Sometimes they contain plant or animal fossils, and sometimes they can help scientists figure out Earth's age and what the environment was like at certain points in time.

Q: That does sound like a nice change from being igneous.

A: Yeah, but for a real change, you can't beat being a metamorphic rock. I mean, that kind of rock's whole NAME means change! Plus, I can become a metamorphic rock without even leaving the underground.

Q: How?

A: There's tons of pressure down there and heat too. That and time is what it takes to squeeze, fold, and flatten until —Sherzam! Granite becomes quartztite. Whole new look. Whole new life. Different shape, hardness, color, shine—and a chance to really be important.

Q: Why do you say that?

A: Metamorphic rocks rule. They give scientists information about what's going on way down in Earth's crust. Geologists can tell Earth's temperature and pressure from studying the metamorphic rocks at different locations.

Q: So what would be your favorite identity?

A: That's a HARD question for a rock to answer. Ha, ha. But I don't really have a favorite, and that's a good thing. I've been all three kinds, and I will be again countless more times. All those changes will happen and happen and happen again. It's called the rock cycle—and it never stops. It's been going on for hundreds of years, thousands of years, millions of years. Rocks have been around forever, which means that I have all the time in the world.

Rockin' Cycle

Rocks can be made over again and again, going back and forth from one type to another in a never ending process called the rock cycle.

Step 1

Minerals are heated to extremely high temperatures and then cooled, forming igneous rocks. When magma cools inside Earth, it forms igneous rocks such as granite. These are called intrusive igneous rocks. And they're coarse-grained because they cool slowly. When lava cools at Earth's surface, it forms igneous rocks such as basalt— a rock with fine grains because it cooled quickly.

Step 2

When rocks are exposed at Earth's surface, their mineral structure changes because they erode and break down into smaller grains. These grains are then transported through wind or water and deposited as sediments, such as sand and pebbles.

Step 3

Sediments are compacted and cemented over time, forming sedimentary rocks. You can usually find sedimentary rocks in and near riverbeds and streambeds. Sedimentary rocks sometimes contain fossils—traces of life—that can give scientists some information about Earth and its past.

Step 4

Igneous or sedimentary rocks that are heated or put under pressure can turn into metamorphic rocks. Some or all of the minerals in the original rocks are replaced, atom by atom, to form new minerals. Metamorphic rocks are often squished, twisted, smeared out, and folded from pressure, water, or heat.

Step 5

At higher temperatures, over time, metamorphic rocks may melt again. That changes the crystals of the rocks and creates igneous rocks. What happens then? Go back to Step 1 and repeat—forever.

Activity

HAWAIIAN HEAT The islands of Hawaii were formed when volcanic lava cooled to form igneous rocks. Use an encyclopedia or the Internet to make a time line of how the islands of Hawaii formed. How has Hawaii's rock composition changed? What type of rocks are found in Hawaii today? Why do you think those rocks are found there? Keeping in mind what you've learned about the rock cycle, what could possibly happen to the igneous islands of Hawaii?

They Keep Glowing, and Glowing, and Glowing

DAY GLOW

Want to shed some light on rocks and minerals? Check out these glowing chunks.

Some rocks and minerals glow under sunlight or a normal light. But you can see serious glowing action when you put certain minerals, like fluorite, under an ultraviolet lamp. Under this lamp, fluorite transforms into a blue–violet color. Why? Because of something called fluorescence, which happens when the mineral's chemicals react with the light, making it glow. Certain electrons in the mineral absorb the light's energy. This kicks the electrons into high gear and gets them glowing. Fluorescence helps scientists identify types of rocks and minerals. And in dark mines or caves, fluorescence can be used to find certain mineral deposits.

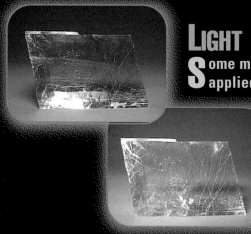

LIGHT ON!

Some minerals keep on glowing—even after the light applied to them is turned off. These minerals are phosphorescent. They store up the light's energy and have an "afterglow" effect. Minerals that phosphoresce are pretty unique, but even more unique are the minerals that don't need anything to glow, like certain types of uranium ores. That's why they're called self-activated minerals.

Break Lights

And if you've ever broken a breath mint in the dark, you know that it emits a flash of light. It's not some bizarre mint power. It's the minerals in the breath mint. The sugar crystals in the mint glow when they're broken or crunched. Hitting two quartz pebbles together in the dark has the same effect. When some minerals get crushed, scratched, or rubbed, they let off a glowing spark. This flashy phenomenon is called triboluminescence.

Heating Up

Other minerals, such as fluorite or calcite, glow when they're heated. That's called thermoluminescence. Thermo comes from the Greek word meaning hot. And when minerals like fluorite get hot, their chemical bonds make them glow. The word "fluorescent" got its name from the glowing mineral fluorite.

Activity

GLOW ON Find some rock specimens from your neighborhood. Bring them into class and expose them to ultraviolet lights (these lights are the types usually used in aquariums). Do any of the rocks glow? If they do, what category of fluorescence do they fit into? Investigate how other types of glow-in-the-dark products work. Are there any similarities between how they glow and how rocks glow?

11

ROCK STARS

What Goes Around...

Even these famous rock sites are composed of one of the three fundamental rock types. Can you determine each type?

	Name	Location	Built by	Key date	Legend
Natural Rock Formations	Ayers Rock	Mount Uluru, Australia	Earth's movement, weathering, and erosion	formed 550 million years ago	Aboriginal people may have lived around Ayers Rock for several thousand years—and they made up a story to explain the rock's formation. One story says the huge rock used to be a flat sandy hill, but battles between tribes turned people into parts of the rock. Women formed the rock's large boulders, and their hair turned into grasses and bushes. Spears used during battles were turned into holes on the cliff face. The rock's red color is attributed to blood.
	Plymouth Rock	Plymouth, Massachusetts	Natural processes	deposited by glaciers 20,000 years ago	Said to have been the first rock Pilgrims set foot on in 1620 when they arrived to the "new world." It was the rock they stepped onto when they stepped off their ship.
	Rock of Gibraltar	Peninsula of Gibraltar	Sedimentation and natural processes	formed 200 million years ago.	The rock is geologically different from its surrounding area. To explain this, people said the ancient Greek god, Hercules, carried the rock to its present site.
Human-made Rock Structures	Parthenon	Athens, Greece	King Pericles asked Phidias, a sculptor, to come up with a sketch of the building. Thousands of people went to work immediately—building the monument by hand.	447 B.C. to 432 B.C.	The monument was built as a shrine to the mythical ancient Greek goddess, Athena. People believed the monument would keep the gods happy.
	Taj Mahal	India	22,000 people over the course of 22 years	1626 to 1648	Shah Jehan, a prince, built this shrine to his wife Mumtaz Mahal, who died three years after he became king. The Taj Mahal is a symbol of Jehan's eternal love for his Mahal.
	Great Pyramid	Ghiza, Egypt	100,000 people working over a 20-year period.	2545 B.C.	The best guess is that the pyramids were built as burial grounds for three kings of Egypt—but no one's 100 percent sure. The Pyramids are considered one of the Seven Wonders of the World.
	Stonehenge	England	Unknown	approximately 2000 B.C. to 1500 B.C.	It's not entirely known why Stonehenge was built. Some say it was used as a calendar and weather predictor, because of the arrangement of the stones in relation to the Sun and Moon. Still another legend states that Merlin, King Arthur's magician, brought the stones from Ireland to England by using his magical powers.

Ancient people didn't have paper, so they wrote on rocks. Rock etchings or carvings are called petroglyphs, and they date back thousands of years. Petroglyphs are found all over the world and are considered to be the first form of written communication. Rocks were used to record events, visions, and storytelling—and today they provide us with the earliest forms of written history. There are so many different types of carvings that it's impossible to completely know what each carving means. But archaeologists have identified the meaning of many common petroglyphs.

Type of rock	Today
Course-grained sandstone rich in the mineral feldspar. The rock is rusty red because the rock also contains iron—an element that rusts.	People go to Ayers Rock seeking adventure. There are lots of caves and holes in the rocks that tourists like to explore. Like other natural rocks, Ayers Rock continues to be affected by weathering and erosion.
granite	Nearly one million people visit Plymouth Rock every year, and it has become a world-famous symbol of courage and faith.
limestone	More than 30,000 people live in Gibraltar—and the rock has come to symbolize the strength of Gibraltar.
marble 	Restoration has been underway for the Parthenon and surrounding ancient monuments since the 1970s. Because of its location directly atop the city of Athens, the building has been degraded by smog and pollution. Tourists flock to Athens to study these ancient marvels.
marble	Tourists visit the Taj Mahal to snap pictures of the beautifully colored monument. 
2.5 million limestone blocks, weighing 2.6 tons each	Visitors head to the spectacular pyramids to marvel at their existence. Weathering and erosion—along with pollution and human actions—have taken their toll on the rocks.
Sarsen stone (sandstone). Each weighs between 4 and 50 tons	While Stonehenge is a major tourist attraction, scientists are still studying the rocky structures to figure out their origin and why they were built.

Largest Crystal:

The largest crystal documented of any mineral is a beryl crystal from Malakialina, Malagasy Republic. It measured 59 feet long (18 meters). It had an estimated volume of 5,050 cubic feet (143 c m) and an estimated weight of 837,748 pounds (380,002 kilograms).

Activity

DIG THIS Grab a friend and make your own rock almanac. Research five other natural rock formations that do not appear in the chart left. Your friend should research five human-made rock structures that do not appear here. On poster board, make a chart like this one and fill in the information. Share your chart with the class and have a rocking good time.

"Gold, Boys, Gold!"

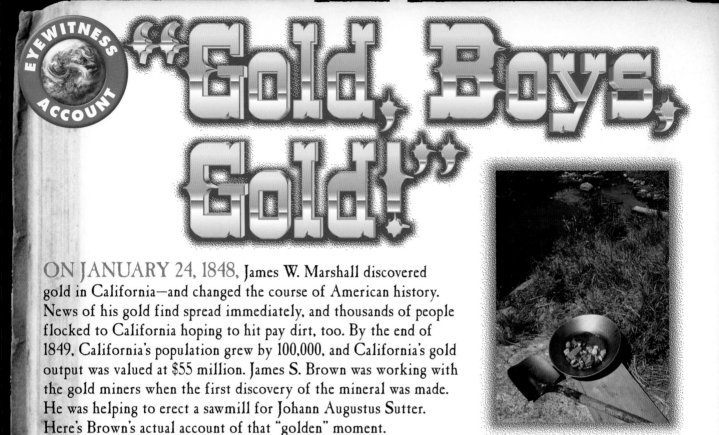

ON JANUARY 24, 1848, James W. Marshall discovered gold in California—and changed the course of American history. News of his gold find spread immediately, and thousands of people flocked to California hoping to hit pay dirt, too. By the end of 1849, California's population grew by 100,000, and California's gold output was valued at $55 million. James S. Brown was working with the gold miners when the first discovery of the mineral was made. He was helping to erect a sawmill for Johann Augustus Sutter. Here's Brown's actual account of that "golden" moment.

January 24, 1848

He [Mr. Marshall] discovered a bed of rock that had been exposed to view by the water the night before; the rock that was in sight was in the bottom of the race [the part below the mill's waterwheel] and was from three to six feet wide and 15 to 20 feet long. It appeared to be granite, but so soft that it might be scaled up with a pick, yet too solid to be carried away by the water.

. . . Mr. Marshall called me to come to him. I went, and found him examining the bed rock. He said, "This is a curious rock, I am afraid that it will give us trouble," and as he probed it a little further, he said, "I believe that it contains minerals of some kind, and I believe that there is gold in these hills." Said I to him, "What makes you think so?" He said he had seen the blossom of gold, and I asked what that was, and he told me that it was the white quartz scattered over the hills. I told him that it was flint rock, but he said no, that it was called quartz in some book that he had read, and that it was an indication of gold. He then sent me to the cabin to bring a pan so that we could wash some of the sand and gravel to see what we could find. On my return we washed some of the sand and gravel and also some of the bed rock that

we scaled up with a pick. As we had no idea of the appearance of gold in its natural state, our search was unsuccessful. Then he said, "Well, we will hoist the gates [of the mill] and turn in all the water that we can to-night, and tomorrow morning we will shut it off and come down here, and I believe we will find gold or some kind of mineral here."

Just when we had got partly to work, here came Mr. Marshall with his old wool hat in hand, and stopped within six or eight yards of the saw pit, and exclaimed, "Boys, I have got her now." I jumped from the pit and stepped to him, and on looking in his hat discovered say ten or twelve pieces of small scales of what proved to be gold. I picked up the largest piece, worth about fifty cents, and tested it with my teeth, and as it did not give, I held it aloft and exclaimed, "Gold, boys, gold!" At that they all dropped their tools and gathered around Mr. Marshall.

Now, having made the first test and proclamation of that very important fact, I stepped to the work-bench and put it to the second with the hammer. While doing that it occurred to me that while in the Mormon Battalion in Mexico, we came to some timber called manzanita. Our guides and interpreters said that wood was what the Mexicans smelted their gold and silver ores with. It is a hard wood and makes a very hot fire and also lasts a long time. Remembering that we had left a very hot bed of these coals in the fireplace of the cabin, I hurried off and made the third test by placing it upon the point of an old shovel blade, and then inserted it in among the coals, and although it was plated almost as thin as a sheet of note paper, the heat did not change its appearance in the least. I remembered hearing that gold could not be burned up, so I arose from this third test confident that it was gold. Then running out to the party who were grouped together, made the second proclamation, saying, "Gold! gold!"

At this juncture all was excitement, and all repaired to the lower end of the tail race, where we found from three to six inches of water flowing over the bed of rock, in which there were crevices and little pockets, over which the water rippled in the glare of the sunlight as it shone over the mountain peaks. James Berger was the first man to spy a scale of the metal. He stooped to pick it up, but found some difficulty in getting hold of it as his fingers would blur the water, though he finally succeeded. The next man to find a piece was H. W. Bigler; he used his jackknife. And as we soon learned how to look for it, as it glittered under the water and in the rays of the sun, we were all rewarded with a few scales. Each put his mite into a small vial that was provided by Marshall, and we made him the custodian. We repeated our visits for three or four mornings to the tail race, each time collecting some more of the precious metal, until we had gathered somewhere between three and four ounces.

There came a rainy day, and it was too wet to work; H. W. Bigler thought it a good day to hunt ducks, so he got on an old coat, and was gone all day. When he returned, we said,"Where are your ducks?" He said, "Wait awhile, I will show you; I have got them all right." Finally he drew an old cotton handkerchief from his pocket, in a corner of which he had at least half an ounce of gold tied up. He said that he had found it down below Sutter's claim, along the river where the bed rock crops out along the bank, and in little rills that come down the hills to the river, and everywhere that he found the bed rock cropping out.

With jack, butcher, and table knives the search was made in the crevices, after stripping the soil from the bed rock with pick and shovel. Next, we conceived the idea of washing the sand and small gravel in time pans, but these were scarce and hard to get hold of. Alexander Stephens dug out a trough, leaving the bottom round like a log. Filling that with sand and gravel that we scraped off the bed rock, he would shake it, having arranged it so as to pour or run water in on the gravel; finally he commenced to rock the trough, which led to the idea of a rocker, which caused the gold to settle at the bottom, and he had it arranged on an incline so that it would naturally not only work to the bottom, but to the lower end of the trough, then at short intervals he would turn it into a tub of water, and at night it would be cleaned and weighed on a pair of wooden scales that he also made, using silver coins for weights, counting the silver dollar equal to one ounce of gold. The rocker above mentioned led to the renowned gold rocker; I am under the impression that Stephens did make the first rocker ever used in California. We made buckskin pouches or wallets to carry the gold in; it was not dust, nor yet nuggets, but small scales.

Activity

FORTY-NINERS TODAY **The gold rush of 1848–1849 was a tremendous historical event. Do some research to learn how the gold rush and the influx of people affected the country and the state. What would happen if gold was discovered in your neighborhood? Write a journal entry about it and describe how people would react and how your life would change.**

Quartz Family
Scrapbook

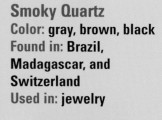

Smoky Quartz
Color: gray, brown, black
Found in: Brazil, Madagascar, and Switzerland
Used in: jewelry

Amethyst
Color: shades of purple
Found in: Brazil, Uruguay, Madagascar
Used in: jewelry, ornaments

Go outside and pick up the first rock you find. Chances are, there's quartz in it. Quartz is the most common mineral on the face of our planet. It makes up about 12 percent of Earth's crust by volume. It's found in almost every type of environment, and it's in almost every type of rock. Why is this mineral everywhere? Quartz dissolves in hot water or steam, so it's easy for it to move around Earth. When the hot fluid cools off or when steam is released, quartz deposits are left. That's why quartz is found at the bottom of streams, on beaches, and in sand.

Quartz comes in lots of different types, colors, and forms, depending on where it was formed and what was going on near the rock at that time. If you pick up a bunch of quartz rocks, you probably won't find any two that look the same. That's good news for rock collectors, who like adding different rocks to their stash.

In its purest form, quartz is colorless and transparent. A clear piece of quartz is called rock crystal. Lots of times, though, quartz is not pure. Impurities mix in with the quartz as the rock is forming. These impurities are responsible for turning quartz into different colors. The size and distinct shape of the crystals tells how quickly the quartz mineral cooled. The slower it cooled, the larger and more beautifully shaped the crystals will be.

Citrine
Color: light yellow to golden brown
Found in:
Brazil, Madagascar, Colorado
Used in: expensive jewelry. Miners and jewelers heat amethyst until it turns yellow or gold to make it citrine.

Rose Quartz
Color: Cloudy pink
Found in: Madagascar, Brazil
Used in: jewelry, because of its rarity

Silicon Valley

Even though quartz is a powerful mineral on its own, when it's mixed with silicon, it packs a potent electrical punch. Combined with silicon, quartz is used in computers, telephones, TVs, stereos, and hand-held computer games.

It's About Time

In 1880, Jacques and Pierre Curie decided to put quartz to the test. They cut a thin slice of quartz and attached a sheet of tin to either side. They hooked up their quartz and tin concoction to a machine that squeezed the tin against the quartz. All that pressure sent small electric charges to the quartz. This phenomenon is called piezoelectricity. *Piezo* means squeeze in Greek, and that's just how the quartz was able to produce electric charges: from the tin's squeeze. In the 1920s, scientists realized that piezoelectricity could be used to keep time. Today, most clocks and watches work because of quartz crystals inside that pulse. If a quartz crystal is charged by a battery, the quartz vibrates more than 32,500 times every second! That's fast!

Making Its Mark

Scientists and rock collectors use something called a Mohs (moze) scale to measure the hardness of a mineral. The scale puts minerals in order from the softest, which is number one, to the hardest, which ranks as number ten. Quartz ranks as seven on the Mohs scale. Say you want to see how hard a certain mineral is. If you scratch quartz against that mineral, and the quartz leaves a mark on the mineral, your mineral is softer than quartz. If quartz doesn't leave a mark, your mineral is harder. You can do the scratch test on any mineral. The softest mineral, or number one on the Mohs scale, is talc, which can be crumbled into a powder. Number ten on the Mohs scale is diamond, which is the hardest mineral around.

Quirky Quartz Beliefs

- Because you can see through a clear quartz crystal, some people think you can see through to the future. Since the middle ages, people have been using clear quartz in crystal balls to predict the future.

- The name quartz comes from the Greek word krustallos, which means ice. Ancient Greeks believed quartz was a nonmelting ice formed by the mythological Greek gods.

- Long ago, people believed that fevers could be cured by placing a piece of quartz on their forehead. They thought it would suck up the heat and cool them off.

- When quartz crystals are rubbed or clicked together, they let off a flash of glowing light. Native Americans rubbed quartz crystals together during ceremonies to simulate lightning.

- People believed that looking at a shining light through a blue quartz crystal could reduce the need to wear glasses.

- Some people believe quartz has amazing healing powers. They say blue or gray quartz helps soothe a sore throat. Rose quartz helps people feel balanced. Copper or yellowish quartz keeps you strong. Clear quartz, they say, can give you love, peace, and harmony, and may even make you psychic.

- Did you know? Quartz is the State Gemstone of Georgia and the State Mineral of Arkansas.

Activity

SCRAP IT **Make a scrapbook of another rock family. Research a rock of your choice to learn more about it. Cut out photographs of the rock and arrange them in your scrapbook. Quiz your human family on the information you find on your rock family.**

Rock Around the World

Some minerals are so rare that they're found in only a few places around the world; others are so common that they can be found almost anywhere. This map shows where newly discovered, rare, and unique minerals are found worldwide.

MICHIGAN Native Americans were the first people to use the Keeweenaw Peninsula for its large amounts of copper.

SOUTH DAKOTA In the Black Hills region, you can find gold and silver, as well as rare and new phosphates.

NEW JERSEY is known as the "fluorescent mineral capital of the world." It's home to old mining areas in the towns of Sterling Hills and Franklin.

CALIFORNIA Boron deposits near Death Valley are the result of hot spring fluids rich in the element boron. When the boron flows into lakes and the water evaporates, it leaves behind borax, which can be used in cleaning agents.

MEXICAN MINING CORRIDOR Copper, lead, silver, gold, and zinc are abundant in the Mexican mining corridor, which stretches from Arizona's border to Mexico City.

ARIZONA At the copper mines in Arizona, you'll find a great assortment of malachite, azurite, turquoise, wulfenite, chrysocolla, cuprite, hemimorphite, and aurichalcite. These minerals are formed in deposits rich in lead, copper, and zinc.

CHILE Minerals can even form in the desert. Chile's Copiapo and Atacama Deserts produce rare halides.

MINAS GERIAS, BRAZIL These mines are brimming with quartz minerals, topaz, aquamarine, and diamonds.

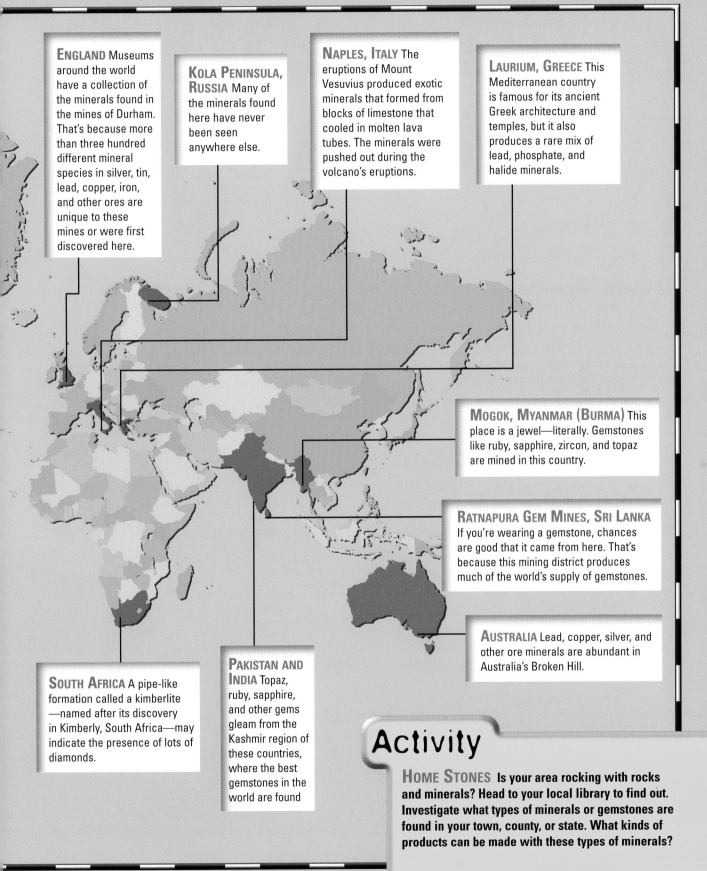

ENGLAND Museums around the world have a collection of the minerals found in the mines of Durham. That's because more than three hundred different mineral species in silver, tin, lead, copper, iron, and other ores are unique to these mines or were first discovered here.

KOLA PENINSULA, RUSSIA Many of the minerals found here have never been seen anywhere else.

NAPLES, ITALY The eruptions of Mount Vesuvius produced exotic minerals that formed from blocks of limestone that cooled in molten lava tubes. The minerals were pushed out during the volcano's eruptions.

LAURIUM, GREECE This Mediterranean country is famous for its ancient Greek architecture and temples, but it also produces a rare mix of lead, phosphate, and halide minerals.

MOGOK, MYANMAR (BURMA) This place is a jewel—literally. Gemstones like ruby, sapphire, zircon, and topaz are mined in this country.

RATNAPURA GEM MINES, SRI LANKA If you're wearing a gemstone, chances are good that it came from here. That's because this mining district produces much of the world's supply of gemstones.

AUSTRALIA Lead, copper, silver, and other ore minerals are abundant in Australia's Broken Hill.

SOUTH AFRICA A pipe-like formation called a kimberlite—named after its discovery in Kimberly, South Africa—may indicate the presence of lots of diamonds.

PAKISTAN AND INDIA Topaz, ruby, sapphire, and other gems gleam from the Kashmir region of these countries, where the best gemstones in the world are found

Activity

HOME STONES **Is your area rocking with rocks and minerals? Head to your local library to find out. Investigate what types of minerals or gemstones are found in your town, county, or state. What kinds of products can be made with these types of minerals?**

POUNDING HEADACHE

GET DOWN!

There's a huge wave coming your way. CRASH! It just washed right over you. And there's another one right behind it. And another one. And another one. And another one. . . .

But you can't get down. You're part of one of the rockiest coastlines in the United States, in northern California. Here, rocky cliffs have been going through this torture for billions of years. And they will continue to undergo it for billions more to come. Massive cliffs get pounded by crashing waves, whipping winds, and burning Sun. Put those all together, and you're suffering from a bad case of erosion.

Erosion wears away the hardest rock, the toughest materials. You try to fight it, but it's no use. As the choppy Pacific Ocean sends waves crashing onto the cliffs, you're worn away. Water can cut through solid rock. Water propelled by the force of waves scours and claws and scrapes.

Actually, for rock, you're not that hard. You're sandstone—soft, crumbly sedimentary rock, like so much of this coastline. Sedimentary rocks are the most damaged by erosion because they're the softest. You have holes, cracks, huge missing pieces. So where have all these pieces gone?

The beach below is a record of your history. It's made mostly of sand particles and rocks—tiny pieces of you and other cliffs around you. The saltwater and force of the waves have broken the cliffs down into smaller particles. As a wave hits the cliff and recedes back into the ocean, it pulls those rock particles right along with it. Some of them get dumped back on the beach when the tide comes in. Fine pieces—or sandy particles—get blown away by wind or washed away by rain.

What's that noise? It sounds like . . . a landslide. Can it be? You bet. Landslides are part of the natural process of coastal erosion—especially in California. The wave that just smashed into a bluff down the coast splintered the soft rock into fragments. Those fragments were

washed away by water, wind, and more. But the landslide didn't happen just because of that one wave. It's been in the making for several months—perhaps years. As harsh winter rains beat down on the cliff, the water penetrated cracks in the rock. Sunlight and wind helped the rock erode, too. All of that loosened up the rock layers and caused the landslide you just witnessed. Rocks and mud tumbled down the cliffs making noise—and a bit of a mess. If the landslide had been bigger, roads, structures, and parts of the beach could have been swept away.

But you're still standing, and so are other rocky faces all around you. None of them have the exact same shape. Some look smoother, some more jagged. There are caves and deep crevices in many of them. That's erosion's work: cutting, smoothing, hollowing, constantly changing the shape of the land. Erosion functions to reduce and level the land until it's all at sea level. So why hasn't Earth eroded to the point where it's completely covered by water? Because erosion has some opposition. Volcanic eruptions and the movements of Earth's crust raise rocks into mountains, plateaus, and new land. That keeps the balance—for the most part. But the coast of California erodes approximately 1 foot (.3 m) every year. Over the next fifty years, parts of California's coast might lose as much as 75 yards (69 m).

You aren't totally alone, however. A specialized community of plants and animals has adapted to the harsh conditions of cliff life. Plant life juts out from holes in your sides. Most cliff soil lacks nutrients for plants, but some soil has collected in ledges, slopes, and cracks. Wind-blown seeds have germinated there resulting in colorful wildflowers in the spring, usually up high, where they're safe from waves. Squawking sea birds are hanging out on ledges that are protected from the waves.

So you do have life. And that's not all. Eroded rock material continues to build up on the beach or in the sea to form loose layers. Over time, those loose layers will fuse and cement together. New land will slowly build up again. That's the part you play in Earth's rock cycle. So all you can do is stand there, look majestic, and take it with a grain of salt.

Activity

NOT BLUFFING Environmental awareness groups and citizens are concerned about the erosion rate of the coastal bluffs in California. Use the Internet to do some research to find out about the factors affecting the coast's erosion. What's being done to help curb the coastline's disappearance? What kind of campaigns and fund-raisers are being held to help save the coast? Have they been successful in raising public awareness?

ROCK OF AGES

Can rocks tell us a story about Earth? Geologist James Hutton—whom people call the father of geology—thought so. And because of Hutton's scientific theories, people now know that rocks are as old as Earth—and some rocks can give us insight as to what kind of life existed on Earth millions of years ago.

In the 1700s, people believed that Earth changed because of major catastrophes, such as floods, and that Earth was born in 4004 B.C. Hutton challenged the geological world with his theory that the land formed and changed because of rock sedimentation, volcanic activity, and erosion. Hutton believed that these processes had been going on for a very long period of time—more than a million years. Geologists in those days said that Earth was only a few thousand years old—and many of them refused to believe Hutton's theory. A popular geologic theory of the time was that land had formed through sedimentation of oceans. But Hutton examined mountains, rocks, and volcanoes to arrive at his theory. In an effort to be heard and understood, Hutton explained his "Theory of the Earth" to the Royal Society of Edinburgh in Scotland, in 1785.

Capital Reef State Park

Scotland, March 4, 1785

The ruins of an older world are visible in the present structure of our planet, and the strata which now compose our continents have been once beneath the sea, and were formed out of the waste of preexisting continents. The same forces are still destroying, by chemical decomposition or mechanical violence, even the hardest rocks, and transporting the materials to the sea, where they are spread out, and form strata analogous [similar] to those of more ancient date. Although loosely deposited along the bottom of the ocean, they become afterwards altered and consolidated by volcanic heat, and then heaved up, fractured and contorted. . . .

We are led . . . to conclude that all the strata of the earth . . . have had their origin at the bottom of the sea, by the collection of sand and gravel, of shells, or coralline and crustaceous bodies, and of earths and clays, variously mixed, or separated and accumulated.

. . . There is, in nature, means employed for the consolidating of strata formed originally of loose and incoherent materials; and that those same means have also been employed in changing the place and situation of those strata [nature has ways of breaking down rocks and putting them into various formation and in various places]. Water could only consolidate strata with such substances as it has the power to dissolve, and having found strata consolidated with every species of substance, it is concluded that strata in general have not been consolidated by means of aqueous solution [rock layers weren't only formed by water, as others had previously believed, because some of the things in the rocks couldn't dissolve in water]. Heat and fusion are found to be perfectly competent for producing the end in view, as every kind of substance may, by heat, be rendered soft, or brought into fusion [heat and pressure causes rocks to break down and fuse layers, or sediments].

Kilauea crater

Grand Canyon

Rock Solid Friends

Hutton's theories were criticized, so his pal Sir James Hall set out to provide evidence for them—and to show that his friend wasn't crazy. Hall conducted at least five hundred experiments to prove Hutton's hypothesis that when rock materials are heated and cooled under high pressure, the materials fuse to form solid rock. One of Hall's experiments was quite strange. He poured powdered chalk into his gun, sealed it shut, heated it up, and let it cool. Then he tipped the gun barrel, and to everyone's surprise—and probably Hall's and Hutton's relief—a marble-like stone came rolling out, proving that the heating and cooling of soft rock materials produce a more solid rock. Hutton also believed that heat from volcanoes was one of the reasons igneous rocks changed form. He was trying to prove that basalt was really an igneous rock and that it was part of rock layers because it had melted and fused into older rocks. But Hutton had never been near an active volcano, so he couldn't prove his theory. Once again, Hall came to the rescue. He conducted experiments to show that the texture of and crystals in melted matter cooled under pressure were the same as the texture of and crystals in basalt—providing support for Hutton's hypothesis that basalt was an igneous rock.

Activity

TAKING THE HEAT Together, Hutton and Hall proved that rocks—and their friendship—can take the heat. Their theories had to be tested and retested in order to prove them correct. Use your imagination: What could have happened if Hall never believed in his friend? How would that have changed the history of geology? What would have been the consequences if they didn't test their hypothesis?

Eat Your ROCKS!

Minerals mean wealth in health. According to the National Science Foundation, your body needs sixty minerals to function healthfully. Minerals for the body are classified into two categories: major and trace. You need more than 100 milligrams of each major mineral every day and fewer than 100 milligrams of trace minerals per day. Where can you find these essential minerals to stay healthy? How about adding some dirt to your meals? Well, not exactly. Minerals are a main ingredient in soil. Plants that grow in the soil suck up minerals through their roots. When animals eat the plants, they're getting a hefty dose of the minerals, too.

Check your lunch bag. Did you pack any minerals? You probably did, without even knowing it. Hopefully, you don't have a basalt and cheese sandwich, but odds are that you do have some kind of mineral wedged between your bread. Here's a typical lunch. Be aware that what's listed here are elements, elements that are parts of the minerals they come from. Listed are the major elements that make up the minerals in the foods. So don't expect to see a piece of copper or iron in your food.

Apple: Boron, calcium, chlorine, copper, iron, magnesium, manganese, nickel, phosphorus, potassium, silicon, sodium, sulfur, vanadium, zinc

Soft Drink: Phosphorus

Sandwich:
❶ **Cheese:** Calcium, phosphorus, potassium
❷ **Tomato:** Chloride, potassium, iron
❸ **Lettuce:** Chloride, silicon, sulfur, cobalt, copper

CROPPING AND CHOPPING

Prehistoric plants were exploding with minerals. That's because thousands of years ago, soil near Earth's surface had a very high mineral content. At least eighty-four minerals were widespread in all soils, and some areas had at least one hundred. Over time though, mineral content in some soil was gradually—and drastically—cut down. As humans began plowing and treating soil to grow crops, the minerals in the soil decreased. Wind and rain also caused minerals to erode from the soil. The result? Some soils now lack several essential minerals which means some plants have fewer minerals—and so do the livestock animals that eat them.

Mineral Magic

What do these minerals do for your body?

Major element of the mineral	What it does:
Boron	Helps out with metabolism.
Calcium	One of the most important minerals. Builds bones and teeth and helps keep your nervous system functioning
Chromium	Helps metabolize glucose, or sugars.
Chlorine	Influences metabolic processes and aids digestion.
Copper, cobalt, zinc	Help enzymes function for metabolism.
Iron	Keeps your muscles—including your heart—running smoothly. It's necessary for making red blood cells, which carry oxygen to every tissue in your body.
Magnesium	Essential for energy production, protein production, and cell growth.
Manganese	Helps bone, tissue, and cell growth.
Nickel	Helps the body use iron better.
Phosphorus	It's an ingredient in many proteins and helps make up cell membranes.
Selenium	Helps develop vitamin E and supports the immune system—so you can fight back against illness.
Silicon	Helps build cartilage and bone.
Sodium and potassium	Helps regulate water levels.
Sulfur	Combines with nitrogen, carbon, and oxygen to form proteins.
Vanadium	May be involved in hormone, glucose, fat, bone, and tooth metabolism, reproduction, and growth.

Milk: Phosphorus, cobalt, zinc, calcium, sulfur

Chocolate bar: Copper

Activity

MINERAL MUNCH What kinds of minerals are in a slice of pizza? Use a nutrition book or go on the Internet to do some research. Then build your own lunch that's full of minerals.

All That Glimmers...

"Hey, guys! Over here!"

"Hey, guys! Over here!" Jake called to his friends. The group was on a mission: They were hunting for unusual rocks to add to their class's rock collection. "I think I found something."

Jake held out the glimmering rock so everyone could see.

"What's that?" Elaine asked, putting on her glasses. "I've never seen anything like it. It's really shiny."

"What does it look like?" Jake said, rolling his eyes. "It's gold, of course!"

"No way!" Dean said, as he snatched the rock from Jake. "Where'd you find it?"

"It was right in front of me, thank you very much!" Jake said and grabbed the rock back. "I dug an inch into the dirt, and there it was, shining up at me, bright as day."

"That's so cool. Do you know what this means?" Elaine asked. "We hit the jackpot! We're rich!" She did a little victory dance.

"Yeah, once we clean this baby up, we'll be the talk of the town!" said Jake. "We'll have a real gold rock to bring to class and add to our rock collection. Ms. Santos will definitely give us an A+. I bet none of her students have ever found gold before!"

Jake rubbed the rock against his jacket. "This must have been sitting here for years," he said. "I guess the rain and snow got to it. I'll take it home and stick it in some jewelry cleaner my mom has. That'll get rid of this rust."

Elaine fished in her pocket for a rock she had found yesterday. "That's even bigger than this rock," she said. "Ms. Santos said my rock was made mostly out of lead. She was pretty impressed that I found such a big piece of lead. Imagine what she'll say when she sees the size of your gold!"

Jake grinned. "Maybe she'll let me take a month off from school! After all, I did find gold!"

Dean eyed Elaine's lead rock. "Can I take a look at that?" he asked.

Elaine tossed it over to him. He studied the rock closely and put it in his palm. "Jake, can I see your rock for a second?"

Jake tossed the rock up in the air. "No way!" But Dean jumped up to get it before Jake had a chance. He rolled the rock around in his hands. "It's about the same weight as Elaine's lead rock," Dean said as he balanced both of them in his palms.

"Hey! Be careful with that thing. I want to make sure it's in perfect shape for tomorrow morning," Jake said. "Once the news of my gold rock spreads, I'll probably be on the front page of every newspaper in town. I'll be rich and famous!"

"I can see the headlines now," Elaine said, motioning in the air. "'The Golden Boy! Boy Hits Pay Dirt! Kid Starts New Gold Rush!'"

Dean wasn't so sure. "I think the newspaper headlines will say, 'Fool Gets Fooled by Gold Rock!'"

"What do you mean?" asked Elaine.

Jake was angry. "He's just jealous because he didn't find the gold first! Well, it's finders, keepers, Dean."

"And losers, weepers, Jake. So you better grab a big box of tissues. Because there's no way this rock is gold!"

How does Dean know?

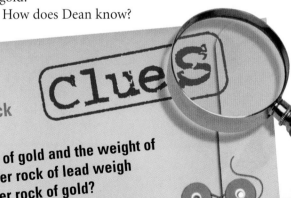

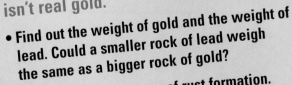

Use these clues to help you figure out why Jake's rock isn't real gold.

- Find out the weight of gold and the weight of lead. Could a smaller rock of lead weigh the same as a bigger rock of gold?

- Investigate the process of rust formation. What causes something to rust? On which minerals or elements does rust form?

Answer on page 32.

Rocking the World

Florence Bascom

Imagine not being able to use the gym or library in your school. Where would you meet your friends for a quick game of soccer? Where would you go to study and do research for reports? That's what happened to college student Florence Bascom in 1877. In those days, female students weren't allowed to enter a school gym, library, or classroom if there were men already in there. But that didn't stop Bascom from studying hard, getting her bachelor's, master's, and doctorate degree—and becoming the first female geologist in the United States.

Perhaps she has her parents to thank. Born in Williamstown, Massachusetts, in 1862, Bascom was the youngest of six children. Her mom, Emma, was a teacher and a leader in the fight for women's right to vote. Bascom's dad, John, supported equal opportunities and rights for women, too. He's the one who encouraged his young daughter to study science and find a career that would make her happy.

When she was fifteen, Bascom was admitted to the University of Wisconsin, where her father was president. Although that may not be such a big deal in today's day and age, it was a big deal in the 1800s. Many colleges and universities absolutely refused to admit female students. But when John Bascom became president of the University of Wisconsin, he changed the school's rules and accepted female students.

Although women were allowed to attend classes, they were not allowed to enter a classroom if the seats were already taken by men. Bascom probably rushed to her classes before any men showed up. All that hard—and unfair—work paid off, though. Bascom got her bachelor's degree in Arts and Letters in 1882. She stayed at the university for two more years to get her bachelor's degree in science. She liked science so much, she decided to turn it into her life's mission. She continued with her studies —and earned her master's degree in geology in 1887. Her father advised her to "make work an immediate joy." And that's exactly what Bascom did.

In 1889, Bascom took graduate school classes at Johns Hopkins University, in spite of the fact that most women still didn't go to college—let alone graduate school. At Johns Hopkins, there was an unusual rule Bascom had to follow: In class, she had to sit behind a screen so male students wouldn't be able to see her and be "disrupted." But Bascom's education was being disrupted by this unfair practice. And the looks she got from fellow male students didn't help either. Bascom might have asked her father for advice on dealing with the situation. He wrote her a letter in September 1891, during

Bascom and company may have studied the rocks during their field trip on this mountain.

rock samples and studied each one in detail, trying to figure out their origin. This research helped Bascom make a landmark discovery. She proved that rocks in the Blue Ridge mountains were not composed of sediment—as other scientists had thought. They were actually metamorphosed lava flows. Her findings gave the geological community new information—and people started paying attention to Bascom and her work.

In 1895, she was asked to go to Bryn Mawr College to teach geology courses. Because geology was only a minor part of the school's science department, Bascom had a lot of hurdles to overcome. Her office—and the entire geology department—consisted of a small storage space, in which she barely had enough room to store books. Over the next two years, Bascom collected hundreds of rocks, minerals, and fossils and amassed a great collection for the geology department. She grew the tiny storage space into a respected geology department.

Other women got wind of Bascom's achievements, and many aspired to be like her. Bascom encouraged young women to study geology, and she trained many other famous and noteworthy female geologists and rock scientists. In the next few decades, Bascom went on to be the first woman to explore many areas of geology. She was the first woman hired

by the United States Geological Survey (1896); she was the first woman to present a paper before the Geological Society of Washington (1901); she was the first woman elected to the Council of the Geological Society of America (1924); and she was the first female officer and vice president of the Society (1930).

But being the first female geologist wasn't the most important achievement in her life. She treasured teaching geology to women more than anything else. In 1931, Bascom wrote a letter to a fellow professor reflecting on her father's advice that work should bring her joy. "I have always claimed that there was no merit in being the only one of a kind," she said. "I have considerable pride in the fact that some of the best work done in geology today by women, ranking with that done by men, has been done by my students . . . these are all notable young women who will be a credit to the science of geology."

her second year of graduate school, advising his daughter: ". . . you better put a stone or two in your pockets to throw at those heads that are thrust out of windows." The advice may have worked. Bascom stayed at the university until 1893 and earned her Ph.D. in geology. She was the second woman in the United States to get a doctorate in that field.

George Huntington Williams, a professor at Johns Hopkins, convinced Bascom to write her doctorate dissertation about the Blue Ridge mountains of Pennsylvania. Bascom spent the summers of 1892 and 1893 in the mountain areas with Williams, studying the mountain's rock formations and crystallization. The two collected thousands of

Florence Bascom contemplates Yellowstone Lake.

What a Gem!

Some minerals are truly gems. Gemstones, that is. Gemstones are specific, rare minerals that form deep in Earth, when pressure and heat change a more common form of the mineral into an extraordinary prize. People have been mining gems such as rubies, diamonds, and sapphires, and using them as jewelry or decorations for centuries. Egyptian emerald mines date back to 1650 B.C., and ancient Egyptians buried gems with their pharaohs to signify wealth. The oldest jewelry ever found comes from 20,000-year-old grave sites.

What makes gems so precious? Besides their beautiful colors, gems are durable. Most can withstand scratching, breakage, and chemical reactions. Gems that are beautiful but scratch easily, such as apatite, are not as prized as stronger minerals, such as diamond. Gems that can be found almost anywhere, such as rock crystal, are called semiprecious. Some gems are called semiprecious because, although they're beautiful, they have some kind of flaw. But the truth is, there is not one gem that is absolutely perfect.

The word "carat" comes from the Greek word keration, which means carob bean. At one time, gems were weighed against piles of carob beans. One carat is approximately the weight of a carob bean: .007 ounce (.2 grams).

The largest diamond ever found was the 3,106 carat Cullinan. Discovered in South Africa in 1905, it was cut into 9 large jewels and 96 smaller ones.

In the seventeenth century, English doctor William Rowland claimed that eating crushed garnets would cure heart problems.

The Birth of Birthstones

▶ **January: Garnet** This gem forms in metamorphic rocks and in some igneous formations. Garnets help geologists figure out how much temperature and pressure the mineral has been through.

Color: mostly red, but comes in a rainbow of colors.

▶ **February: Amethyst** In Greek, the word amethyst means "not drunk." Maybe that's why people believed that amethyst could ward off alcohol's effects. But the name probably came from the mineral's wine-purple color. The best amethyst minerals are formed in gas cavities in volcanic rocks in India, Uruguay, and Brazil.

Color: range of purple shades.

▶ **March: Aquamarine** Just like it's name implies, aquamarine is aqua colored, or blue like the sea. It's made from the mineral beryl, which forms in granites, pegmatites, and schists. In the United States, this gem is found in California and Utah. To get the deep blue color, most yellow or pale aquamarine stones are heated.

Color: blue-green.

▶ **April: Diamond** Why does a diamond last forever? It's the hardest of all known minerals and can stand up to almost anything. Because diamonds form deep within Earth's crust in igneous rocks, miners usually have to dig up 500 tons (454 tonnes) of ore just to get one ounce of diamond. Most diamonds are used in industry; only a special few make their way to jewelry stores.

Color: clear, white, pink. The most rare is the red diamond.

▶ **May: Emerald** Like March's birthstone, emerald comes from the mineral beryl. But the green color is made from small amounts of chromium and iron. Most emerald crystals are slightly cracked, but that doesn't mean they're not good. Breaks in this gem show that the emerald is real.

Color: deep green.

▶ **June: Pearl** This is the only birthstone that's not a rock. Natural pearls are made when a shellfish, such as an oyster, gets a grain of sand caught inside its shell. To protect itself, the shellfish secretes a material that wraps around the sand and hardens into a pearl. Because that process takes a while, pearl farmers insert a small bead into an oyster to produce a bigger pearl faster.

Color: pink, green, blue, white, black.

▶ **July: Ruby** Rubies and sapphires come from the mineral corundum, but trace amounts of the mineral chromium make a ruby red. Corundum is the second hardest natural mineral known to mankind. Ruby is formed in metamorphic rocks and can also be found as deposits in riverbeds.

Color: pink to red.

▶ **August: Peridot** This gem is out of this world! It's sometimes found in meteorites, though it mostly is found in lava and deep igneous rocks. It's composed of the mineral olivine. Because it's not as green as an emerald, it's sometimes called the "poor-man's emerald." But legend has it that it was Cleopatra's favorite gemstone.

Color: various shades of green.

▶ **September: Sapphire** Like rubies, sapphire comes from the mineral corundum. But iron and titanium give it its color. Unlike rubies, which are formed in flat crystals, sapphires form a barrel or pyramid shape.

Color: blue, orange-pink, golden, white, yellow, mauve, clear, black.

▶ **October: Opal** Opal forms over long periods of time in sedimentary rocks, but it's also found in volcanic rocks in Mexico and Czechoslovakia. There's water in opal and, depending on how much, geologists can figure out the temperature of the rock at the time the opal formed.

Color: blue, green, yellow, and red rainbow; black, white, milky, red.

▶ **November: Topaz** Topaz is a heavy-duty gem. Its crystals can be very large and reach several hundred pounds. It's also among the hardest minerals in nature, which is one of the reasons this gem has been used in jewelry for centuries.

Color: yellow, pink, multicolored, and blue, which is produced by heating clear topaz crystals.

▶ **December: Turquoise** Egyptians have mined this gem since 6000 B.C., and it's been used in jewelry for more than three thousand years. Its name comes from a French word meaning "stone of Turkey," the country through which this stone passed to get to Europe. Turquoise is also found in New Mexico, Arizona and Nevada, accumulating in crevices of slate and sandstone. The color is so unique that the mineral's name is commonly used to describe a green-blue color.

Color: greenish blue.

Earth is so rocky, it's been dubbed the "third rock from the Sun." But Earth is not the only body in the Solar System that contains rocks. Scientists have been studying rock and mineral material from other planets, especially Mars.

Why study these far-out rocks called meteorites? Because meteorites can tell a story about when and how the Solar System was formed. They help explain the atmosphere of the planet they came from and give us clues about Earth's history. For the past few years, scientists have been studying meteorites for signs of life on other planets—especially Mars. One famous Martian meteorite, Rock 84001, has made headlines because of possible evidence that shows there's possible microscopic life on Mars.

Gather friends or classmates around and:

One: Research newspaper clippings and scientific journals for information about Rock 84001 and other Martian meteorites.

Two: Form two teams to debate the evidence of the Martian rock. What are the implications if this rock is a definite link to life on Mars? How can scientists use this information for the future? Why is so much work being done to learn more about meteorites? Do you think scientists should study meteorites to learn about life on other planets?

Three: Within your teams, work with a partner. Pretend one of you is the head scientist in the quest for life on Mars. Using your research on the Martian meteorites, write a document explaining why the search for life on Mars should continue. Include possible evidence and its implications. Your partner is against looking for life on Mars. This scientist believes the information found thus far doesn't prove there's life out there, so the meteorite project should be halted in order to conserve money and time. Write a document defending this position against the further study of Martian meteorites.

Four: Debate your position in class. Allow the audience to ask questions and try to answer them as soon as possible. Have the class vote based on the strength of your arguments.

Five: Write up the results and share them with other classes.

Think About This:

❶ In the past thirty years, more than ten thousand meteorites have been found in Antarctica. NASA and other agencies have teamed up to develop a robot that hunts down meteorites in Antarctica. The robot, called the Nomad Rover, helps scientists working in Antarctica track down and positively identify meteorites trapped in ice. Why is so much work being done to learn more about meteorites?

❷ Lunar rocks, brought back from the Apollo mission to the Moon, provided scientists with a wealth of information about Earth and its Moon. How did the lunar rocks change the way people thought about the Moon, Earth, and the Solar System?

❸ Scientists say life on Earth began from a single microscopic organism. If that's the case, what does this find say about Mars?

ANSWERS Solve-It-Yourself Mystery, pages 26–27:

1. A smaller rock of lead could not weigh the same as a bigger rock of gold because gold has a greater density.

2. Gold does not rust. Rust forms in minerals containing iron.